Mending Fences

The Kuyper Lecture Series

The annual Kuyper Lecture is presented by the Center for Public Justice in cooperation with leading institutions throughout the country. The lecture seeks to enlarge public understanding of three dynamics at work in the world today: the driving influence of competing religions in public life, the comprehensive claims of Jesus Christ on the world, and the strength of the Christian community's international bonds. The lecture is named in honor of Abraham Kuyper (1837–1920), a leading Dutch Christian statesman, theologian, educator, and journalist.

The Center for Public Justice is an independent, nonprofit organization that conducts public policy research and pursues civic education programs, such as the Kuyper Lecture, from the standpoint of a comprehensive Christian worldview. The Center advocates equal public treatment of all faiths and seeks political reforms to strengthen the diverse institutions of civil society.

Each book in the Kuyper Lecture series presents an annual Kuyper Lecture together with the responses given to it.

Books in the Kuyper Lecture Series

Mark A. Noll, *Adding Cross to Crown: The Political Significance of Christ's Passion,* with responses by James D. Bratt, Max L. Stackhouse, and James W. Skillen (the 1995 lecture).

Calvin B. DeWitt, *Caring for Creation: Responsible Stewardship of God's Handiwork,* with responses by Richard A. Baer Jr., Thomas Sieger Derr, and Vernon J. Ehlers (the 1996 lecture).

Dan Coats, *Mending Fences: Renewing Justice between Government and Civil Society,* with responses by Glenn C. Loury, Mary Nelson, and Stanley W. Carlson-Thies (the 1997 lecture).

Mending Fences

*Renewing Justice between Government
and Civil Society*

Dan Coats

with responses by

Glenn C. Loury

Mary Nelson

Stanley W. Carlson-Thies

edited by James W. Skillen

The
Center
for Public
Justice
P.O. Box 48368
Washington, D.C. 20002

Baker Books
A Division of Baker Book House Co
Grand Rapids, Michigan 49516

© 1998 by The Center for Public Justice

Published by Baker Books
a division of Baker Book House Company
P.O. Box 6287, Grand Rapids, MI 49516-6287

Printed in the United States of America

Library of Congress Cataloging-in-Publication Data

Coats, Daniel R., 1943–
    Mending fences : renewing justice between government and
civil society / Daniel R. Coats : with responses by Glenn C. Loury,
Mary Nelson, Stanley W. Carlson-Thies ; edited by James W.
Skillen.
        p. cm. — (The Kuyper lecture series)
    ISBN 0-8010-5830-9 (pbk.)
        1. United States—Social conditions—1980– 2. United States—
Social policy—1993– 3. United States—Politics and government—
1993– 4. Social justice—United States. 5. Civil society—United
States. I. Loury, Glenn C. II. Skillen, James W. III. Title. IV. Series.
HN65.C58 1998
306'.0973—dc21   98-23846

For current information about all releases from Baker Book House, visit our web site:
                        http://www.bakerbooks.com

Contents

Foreword

James W. Skillen

Politics and government appear in a different light today than they did just a few decades ago. Those who argue for less government and more market freedom have the upper hand. Throughout the world, liberal democracy is lauded and communism is dead.

Yet not all is well with human society. Early in 1998 the American economy is growing, with employment high and interest rates low, but there is more to human well-being than a vibrant economy. The poorest of the poor seem to be locked into permanent hopelessness and, relatively speaking, are becoming poorer every day. American society in general, as measured by divorce rates, out-of-wedlock births, quality of television programming, and civic duty, is not very healthy.

Senator Dan Coats (R-Ind.) applauds economic prosperity and a more limited role for government. He is distressed,

James W. Skillen has been the executive director of the Center for Public Justice and editor of the Center's *Public Justice Report* since 1981. A frequent speaker both in the U.S. and abroad, he is also a widely published author. His books include *Recharging the American Experiment: Principled Pluralism for Genuine Civic Community* (Grand Rapids: Center for Public Justice; Baker, 1994) and *The Scattered Voice: Christians at Odds in the Public Square* (Grand Rapids: Zondervan, 1990).

however, by the moral crisis of the culture and particularly by the signs of a weakening "civil society"—the web of society's nongovernment institutions. This was the topic he chose to address on October 30, 1997, when he gave the third annual Kuyper Lecture, sponsored by the Center for Public Justice in cooperation with Wheaton College (Ill.).

The difficulty we face today, he said, is that the American republic was founded on a concept of freedom that requires individual self-discipline and virtue, and if the institutions of civil society do not train people to become good and virtuous citizens, liberal democracy cannot work. There is actually a paradox here, according to Senator Coats: "America is a liberal country that relies on the vitality of conservative institutions to teach the moral habits of democracy that keep us a liberal country." By "liberal country," he means a republic that does not impose moral absolutes on people in public life. By "conservative institutions," he means family, church, and other nongovernment entities that may and must use moral authority to shape citizens.

Senator Coats accepts this paradox inherent in the viewpoint of America's founders. Consequently, given his concern with the moral crisis of American society, his aim as a legislator, first in the House of Representatives and now in the Senate, has been to seek means of strengthening the authority as well as the economic well-being of those institutions that teach moral virtues. This is a difficult job, he says, because "if moral absolutes are imposed on public institutions, we sacrifice freedom," but on the other hand if public relativism and individualism "undermine the authority and power of civic institutions to shape moral citizens," democracy cannot be maintained.

The senator's approach has been to try to use government's authority to encourage morally constructive actions in the nongovernment sector by, for example, proposing a charity tax credit that would give taxpayers the opportunity to direct some of their tax dollars to private charities. Senator Coats does not believe government can reconstruct civil society directly; that would be a contradiction in terms. On the other hand he does not believe, as many conservatives do, that simply by reducing government and letting the market take over, virtuous citizens and a healthy democracy will result.

At the core of Senator Coats's legislative agenda has been his Project for American Renewal, made up of almost two dozen proposals that he hopes will encourage parents, church leaders, nonprofit service providers, and others to act on their moral and religious convictions. Government ought not to impose one set of convictions, he says, but neither should it stand in the way of citizens acting firmly on their moral and religious convictions. Government policies should not convey indifference or moral relativism. We do not want "a democracy of values in which every belief is equally true, equally false, and equally meaningless."

The challenge for Senator Coats arises from the paradox that he so ably describes. If he tries to use public law to restrict pornography on the Internet or television, for example, does he not come down on the side of asking government to enforce one set of moral values to the exclusion of others? Is that the proper task of liberal government? If on the other hand such restrictions are essential to encourage authoritative moral responsibility on the part of families, schools, and the broadcast media, should he not seek such restrictive legislation even if many citizens disagree with his moral values?

The three respondents to Senator Coats pick up on this dilemma. Glenn C. Loury, professor of economics and director of the Institute on Race and Social Division at Boston University, suggests that the cultural roots of contemporary relativism are deeper than the senator may realize. Loury doubts that the legislative approach Senator Coats has in mind will do much to encourage the regeneration of civil society. Precisely because the responsibilities in question are personal, moral, and spiritual, public law in the form of tax incentives and "moral scolding" will not go far. The senator expects too much from government's action. "I am also ambivalent," says Loury, "about a vision that sees the churches as primary instruments of social-service provision." The church "should be about spiritual business."

Mary Nelson, president of Bethel New Life, a multifaceted, Christian community-development ministry in Chicago, responds to Senator Coats from a different angle. If he is seriously concerned about human moral recovery, she says, he should be advocating even more the use of government initiatives to encourage social and economic reform. Senator Coats does not say enough about justice, in Nelson's estimation. He does not stress the Judeo-Christian tradition's concern with the common good of the whole community, and he underestimates the moral and religious importance of government's actions to "unite things such as land planning, public transportation, health care, taxation for education, and so forth."

Stanley W. Carlson-Thies, director of social-policy studies at the Center for Public Justice, suggests Senator Coats can find an answer to the founders' paradox as well as to Loury and Nelson by digging deeper into the political vision of Abraham Kuyper, whom the senator quotes near the end of his address. American Christians should not simply accept the paradox of the founders' ideology. That framework requires criticism from a position above it. Carlson-Thies says it is too limiting to define the appropriate role of government in civil society as one of empowering nongovernment groups by steering public monies to them. "The divine call to government to promote justice requires more robust action than this." Government is more than a facilitator and protector of freedom. It has its own moral responsibility to advance and uphold the well-being of the public trust, the commonwealth, the just order of society.

Government cannot produce spiritual and moral revival, to be sure; it must not seek to reconstruct society on its own as a totalitarian authority. At the same time, its responsibility to establish justice amounts to more than upholding the moral authority of nongovernment organizations. Carlson-Thies, following Kuyper, argues that government's task of doing justice is itself a moral responsibility. This is something that the liberal tradition does not recognize. Government in its own sphere, as well as families, schools, churches, businesses, and a wide variety of other social institutions, all have distinct responsibilities that together must be fulfilled to make possible the common good. Recognizing and seeking to strengthen this diverse range of human moral responsibilities offers a way out of the founders' paradox.

Senator Coats and respondents Glenn Loury, Mary Nelson, and Stanley Carlson-Thies outline in brief compass one of the greatest public challenges for Christians in our day: how to use all the resources of the Christian faith to approach all aspects of human responsibility in this world in ways that will allow us to exercise proper responsibility in every sphere of life. Christianity requires a critical reappraisal of all habits and ideologies. Mending fences should take place in the light of God's revelation, which comes through the order of creation and in Christ's recovery of the sinfully distorted creation by his redeeming grace.

The Hopes and Fears of America's Founders

★

At this moment of history people throughout the world are inspired by the hopes of America's founders. But we should also be instructed by their fears.

In 1819 John Adams wrote to Thomas Jefferson, asking, "Will you tell me how to prevent riches from being the enemy of industry? Will you tell me how to prevent luxury from producing intoxication, extravagance, vice and folly?"

When the founders turned from dreaming to worrying, they worried about this: How could a free and prosperous people preserve a moral culture? How could a commercial republic, celebrating individual liberty and personal gain, cultivate concern for the common good and moral restraint? Would the spirit of freedom undermine the habits of character that make freedom noble and possible?

These concerns grew out of a carefully constructed worldview—a comprehensive vision of man and the state.

The Founders' Ideology

Though our republic was designed to preserve liberty, the founders believed this requires a certain kind of citizenry—

citizens not of perfect Christian virtue but with democratic habits and manners. Reasoned reflection. Self-mastery. Public spirit. A respect for the rights of others. These democratic virtues would temper and check our political and economic systems. They would promote obedience to laws out of choice, not fear; they would encourage the pursuit of happiness over the pursuit of mere pleasure; they would promote a kind of politics that serves public goals and not private advantage.

Professor Gordon Wood, in *The Creation of the American Republic,* describes the common belief of America's founders. "Every state in which the people participated needed a degree of virtue; but a republic which rested solely on the people absolutely required it. . . . Only with a public-spirited, self-sacrificing people could the authority of a popularly elected leader be obeyed, but 'more by the virtue of the people, than by the terror of his power,' because virtue was truly the lifeblood of the republic."

It follows from this view that the forms of democratic government—its checks, balances, and rules—are not sufficient. Samuel Adams wrote, "Neither the wisest constitution nor the wisest laws will secure the liberty and happiness of a people whose manners are universally corrupt." Democracy in this view is a set of habits, not a set of institutions. It depends on an internalized willingness to respect the rights and dignity of others. "Constitutions," said Fisher Ames, our bluntest founder, "are but paper; society is the substratum of government."

The founders, for example, would not have been surprised that Weimar Germany had a carefully written, democratic constitution with ample checks and balances, even though the German republic ended in the election of a totalitarian tyrant. It was the democratic virtues of German citizens that failed, not their constitution.

In the worldview of the founders, civic education—education in the democratic virtues—assumes a central importance. Citizens are not born; they are cultivated. Civility, deliberation, and consensus building are learned behaviors—and not easily learned. These virtues require more than intellectual assent; they must take root not only in minds but in hearts. Character development is necessary precisely because it secures freedom.

The founders assumed that one of the instruments of civic education would be religion, the carrier of conscience. So they made the effort to celebrate faith, even when they did not share it. John Adams was not a churchman and might even be described as a secularist. But he wrote, "One great advantage of the Christian religion is that it brings the great principle of the law of nature and nations, love your neighbor as yourself, and do to others as you would have that others should do to you—to the knowledge, belief and veneration of the whole people. Children, servants, women, and men are all professors in the science of public as well as private morality. . . . The duties and rights of the man and the citizen are thus taught from early infancy."

Finally, the founders sensed a tension between this spirit of religion and the spirit of freedom or democracy. Adams worried aloud that "commerce, luxury, and avarice have destroyed every republican government." Ames concluded, "A democratic society will soon find its morals an encumbrance . . . the surly companion of its licentious joys." They feared that citizens, who accepted freedom as the goal of their government and their economy, might come to accept freedom as the goal of their lives. But freedom as a moral goal is empty because it can lead to the internal tyranny of appetites and self-interest. And this in the founders' view would weaken the supports of democracy itself. They agreed with Edmund Burke: "Men of intemperate mind never can be free. Their passions forge their fetters."

This is a hard teaching, and it makes many modern Americans uncomfortable. The founders were saying in essence that self-government is possible only when citizens can gov-

ern themselves. Freedom requires that citizens broadly share
some vision of what is right and good—reciprocity, tolerance, compassion. Without these things democracy loses its
legitimacy. Irving Kristol summarizes the founders' conviction: "There is no inherent right to self-government if it
means that such government is vicious, mean, squalid and
debased." As I said, a hard teaching.

The Art of Association

In many ways American society succeeded beyond the
expectations of the founders. We discovered rich supplies of
democratic virtue, and not just in the well-born, the edu-
cated, the landed. We found those virtues in immigrants,
freed slaves, and women, places the founders might not have
expected. And the explanation leads us to Alexis de Tocqueville, the French aristocrat who became a founder by adop-
tion, completing their worldview.

Democratic virtues were common in America, Tocqueville
observed, because we had perfected the art of association.
In a nine-month-long tour during the administration of An-
drew Jackson, Tocqueville found strong families, workers associations, educational institutions, neighborhoods, town
governments, religious groups—a profusion of institutions
that stand between individuals in their private lives and large
institutions of public life. And all of them in one way or another served the cause of civic education, instructing citizens
in the use of freedom. "Local institutions," Tocqueville wrote,
"are to liberty what primary schools are to science; they put
it within the people's reach; they teach people to appreciate
its peaceful enjoyment and accustom them to make use of
it. Without local institutions a nation may give itself a free
government, but it has not got the spirit of liberty."

These institutions protect against government centraliza-
tion and tyranny by creating a zone of organization, authority, and action outside politics. But they also protect against

individualism, turning our attention to the needs of others, the benefits of cooperation, the necessity of trust, and the value of the common good. And they teach us true toler-ance—accepting differences without division. Sociologist Alan Wolfe explains that these institutions are valuable "not because they create havens in an otherwise heartless world, but because it can only be within the intimate realm, sur-rounded by those we know and for whom we care, that we learn the art of understanding the moral positions of others."

Like the founders, Tocqueville worried about how the spirit of equality and democracy would affect individual character and the associations he celebrated. In an "age of equality," he said, "private interest will more than ever be-come the chief if not only driving force behind all behavior." He warned that materialism would "enervate the soul and noiselessly unbend its springs of action." And he described a democratic development called "individualism," what he called "a word unknown to our ancestors." This was his def-inition: "A calm and considered feeling which disposes each citizen to isolate himself from the mass of his fellows." It can result in a situation, he said, in which "each man is forever thrown back on himself alone, and there is danger that he may be shut up in the solitude of his own heart."

In Tocqueville's view civic education—freeing individu-als from the solitude of their selfishness—is one of democ-racy's most urgent tasks. He warned that if democratic na-tions should fail in "imparting to all citizens those ideas and sentiments which first prepare them for freedom and then allow them to enjoy it, there will be no independence left for anybody . . . neither for the poor nor for the rich, but only an equal tyranny for all."

The Paradox of the American Experiment

Even the briefest survey of the founders' writings reveals the existence of an American ideology: republican government sustained by republican virtue. But most people do not understand the paradox at the heart of this belief. In this view the survival and success of liberal public institutions, oriented toward liberty, choice, and tolerance, depend directly on the health of nonliberal or conservative institutions, emphasizing authority, limits, and moral absolutes. The endurance of civil liberties depends directly on schools, churches, volunteer associations, neighborhoods, and families that shore up the old democratic decencies. The ACLU and the Christian Coalition, whether they recognize it or not, are both part of the same communal enterprise. We only find freedom on the other side of obedience and duty. Liberty is meaningless without law.

Let me state the paradox once again: America is a liberal country that relies on the vitality of conservative institutions to teach the moral habits of democracy that keep us a liberal country.

The American experiment is thus conducted on a tightrope. If moral absolutes are imposed on public institutions, we sacrifice freedom. The founders had no patience for oppressive governments and established churches. But the equal or greater danger was that liberalism, relativism, individualism, materialism—the spirit of freedom and democracy—would undermine the authority and power of civic institutions to shape moral citizens who are prepared for freedom. And this places government in particular in a delicate position. It cannot impose by force or fiat the virtues on which it depends. But it cannot ignore the health or sickness of the communities in which those virtues are instilled. So the founders leave us with a challenge: How can we nurture the virtue of a free nation and still leave it free?

An illustration used by Michael Novak makes this point. He asks us to examine the Statue of Liberty. "Look at the statue closely. It is the figure of a woman, in French iconography the symbol of wisdom, in her uplifted hand the torch of reason warding off the mists of passion and ignorance; in her other hand, the Book of the Law. Liberty in this representation is ordered liberty, liberty under the sway of reason, liberty under law. This is not, Lord Acton said, the liberty to do as one wishes; it is the liberty to do what is right."

This is the form of liberty the founders wanted to encourage, without oppression but also without apology.

The Founders' Fears Revisited

★

In the modern world of political ideas, it is amazing how uniformly and how universally the ideology of the founding has been abandoned. It is a dead language, like Latin, studied by a few experts, seldom spoken in public. In fact, the object of much modern political thought has been to refound the American republic without reference to virtue.

On one side of the spectrum, libertarians seek to elevate liberty to an absolute value—a goal served by the voluntary interaction of markets and undermined by the compulsion of government. They argue that the absolute freedom to do as we please will automatically result in a just society because the just society is defined as the absolute freedom to do as we please. Virtue may be privately comforting, but it is publicly irrelevant, they say, because markets can get along on self-interest alone. And public life, in an ideal world, would be nothing more than the operation of free markets.

On the other side, modern liberals embrace government but often only when it is used to secure individual rights, to restrain the free exercise of the market, with the goal of economic parity, and to guarantee individual choice. Government exists, they say, to respect those choices, to expand them when possible, and to stay strictly neutral between them. So, for example, out-of-wedlock birth and divorce become options on an infinite menu of valid lifestyles, viewed as individual decisions government is supposed to protect from prejudice, not condemn or discourage. And formulation of the common good involving morality—"Divorce should be discouraged" or "Illegitimacy hurts children"—is a threat to individual rights. Moral judgment by government is thus seen as identical to political oppression.

Both viewpoints come under the descriptive label "procedural democracy." Procedures—legal and economic rules that guarantee individual liberty—are all that count. And that liberty is defined as freedom from any imposed system of values, as the total freedom of autonomous will. "At the heart of liberty," according to Supreme Court Justices Sandra Day O'Connor, David Souter, and William Kennedy in a recent majority decision, "is the right to define one's own concept of existence, of meaning, of the universe, of the mystery of human life." This is a breathtaking shift. In two centuries we have gone from liberty under law to an unqualified individual right to define the meaning of the cosmos.

In this worldview, government has nothing to say about the character of its citizens, since to favor one moral ideal above another would be elitist. In the process the goal of civic education is transformed. Education in democratic virtues is seen as quaint at best, intolerant at worst. In its place there must be instruction of the young in a relativistic tolerance for the moral choices of other citizens, a tolerance defined as endorsement. The private conduct of citizens is simply irrelevant to the public order of rights and laws. It is, in T. S. Eliot's phrase, a system so perfect that no one needs to be good.

The Need for Virtue

Yet in the last few decades there have been growing doubts about the perfection of this system. And those questions have resulted not from philosophic reflection but from human suffering. It has become evident, for example, that the lifestyle choice of casual divorce by adults has destructive consequences in the lives of children, making them prone to violence, depression, suicide, educational failure, sexual aggression, and drug abuse. Clearly there is a conflict here between the rights of adults to define their "own concept of existence" and our duties to the fragile emotional world of childhood. Clearly there is a problem when the liberty of some citizens leaves scars in the lives of others. The same point could be made concerning illegitimacy, which for men represents an exercise in sexual license and for mothers and children becomes a burden that demands daily heroism to hold together a normal life. Similar arguments could be made regarding sexual liberty that leads to disease, or alcohol use that leaves carnage on the roads, or gambling that breeds addiction and disrupts families, or academic cheating so commonplace that it makes a sham of education.

When these moral choices are rare, isolated, and punished by stigma, they remain private matters, private tragedies. But when these moral choices are prevalent and threaten to dissolve the norm, when 70 percent of children will spend some time in a broken home, or when in some communities 90 percent of births are illegitimate, these private tragedies gather into major social problems, complicating the lives of every citizen, clouding the moral judgment of children, leading them into the dark valley of an empty life. After decades of "liberation" from traditional norms, community expectations, and family obligations—all obstacles to personal freedom and self-expression—there are countless voices to testify in the indictment of our times. A child whose life is haunted by the betrayal of a father; a young person under the death sentence of a sexual disease; a woman in the poverty and loneliness of abandonment—together these might ask, Where is my liberty in this system of ab-

solute liberty? Where is my freedom, which has been tram-
pled by the limitless freedom of others?

It is increasingly clear that the quality of our lives as citizens depends on the character of our neighbors as human
beings, on their ability and willingness to conform their exercise of liberty to a set of moral rules. Every society depends directly and permanently on the intention of most
citizens at most times to be good—not perfect but good.
"The most important change in how we define the public
interest in the last 20 years," observes Professor James Q.
Wilson, "has been a deepening concern for the development of character in the citizenry." As an example, he
points to a study by Professor Travis Herschi on the causes
of juvenile delinquency. Herschi took as his question not
why some people commit crimes but why most people
obey the law. He isolated four key elements by observing
children in Richmond, California. Children obey the law
because they are attached to their family; because they appreciate the cost of wrong actions and the benefits of right
ones; because they are involved in conventional activities
such as school; and because they believe in the moral va-
lidity of society's rules.

This describes an older form of civic education, the kind
that would have been familiar to Tocqueville. The goal is to
create not saints but orderly, law-abiding citizens. The prerequisites for this job are stable institutions—churches, families, schools, and voluntary associations—that instill a belief in a hierarchy of moral values, along with a conviction
that in the long run an individual is better off in a morally
ordered society. When this kind of teaching is consistent and
sustained, the result is a set of moral habits, not merely moral
beliefs. Aristotle said, "We become just by doing just acts,
temperate by doing temperate acts, brave by doing brave
acts." It is the little moments that shape the vital hours. And
it is in the value-shaping institutions of civil society that we
turn convictions into character.

America's Mixed Blessings

We are rediscovering the central importance of these institutions to democracy at the very moment when they are
under unprecedented assault. Great forces in our society,
forces that unleash individualism and disrupt social con-
vention, are making civic education more difficult, complicating the creation of virtuous citizens. But in this case there
are no easily identified enemies, because those same forces
have also created wealth and propelled social progress. They
have undermined American character and built American
greatness. They are a mix of light and shadow, the cursed
blessings of American life.

Government

The first of these mixed blessings is government, particularly the federal government. It is simple blindness to deny
that our central government has grown in large part because
of a momentum of achievement. In fifty years it saved the
world and liberty itself from two totalitarian states, sponsored the Manhattan Project and the Apollo program,
granted voting and other civil rights to African-Americans,
and delivered millions of the elderly from destitution. In 1960
senior citizens were the largest group in poverty. After thirty
years of Social Security and Medicare, they are now the
smallest.

But it is also impossible to deny that the size and reach of
our government have adversely influenced the character of
democracy and the nature of citizenship. It is an extraordi-
nary thing how far we have come. At the beginning of the
Jackson administration, about the time Tocqueville made
his American tour, the entire federal government, excluding
Congress and the military, for a population of 12.5 million
people consisted of 352 individuals. A little earlier, in 1815,
President Madison paid a single secretary out of his own

pocket, and the Supreme Court met for two months a year in a boardinghouse. In America today there are 18.6 million full- and part-time employees at all levels of government, one for every seventeen people. Ten percent of our gross domestic product goes to creating and enforcing federal government regulations.

There is little doubt that this expansion has come at a cost, what has been called the Faustian bargain of American social policy: trading our spirit for sustenance. In a democracy, public power is a zero-sum game. When government takes more, citizens retain less. Centralized power has often replaced communities and families and discouraged community participation, thus weakening the skills of self-government. And particularly when fighting poverty, it has subsidized self-destructive behavior, sent perverse moral messages, and encouraged habits of dependence, reducing citizens to serfs.

I have seen firsthand how a well-intentioned government can treat living communities as the playthings of utopian planners. After my undergraduate work at Wheaton College, I joined a Chicago consulting firm whose purpose was to implement President Lyndon Johnson's Great Society programs. One of my tasks was to go door to door in poor neighborhoods, convincing residents it was a good thing that their houses were to be condemned and bulldozed to make way for high-rise public housing. I showed them pictures of the clean, new apartments with modern elevators. But many of them protested and even wept when hearing the news because, to my astonishment, they loved their homes and the decayed neighborhood around them. Of course, none of this really mattered, since they had to go anyway. Our good intentions required it. It turned out, of course, that they were right. Their homes and neighborhoods, as bad as they were, were living communities, a place of family and sanctuary. Our government high-rises turned out to be sterile, impersonal, and soulless. In the years since, they have become unworthy of human habitation, a shame to our nation and a symbol of the destructive potential of goodness without wisdom. My experience in those homes and neighborhoods profoundly shaped my view of government and politics.

Tocqueville the philosopher was also Tocqueville the prophet. He described how government action, the result of democracy, could enfeeble democracy.

> What political power could ever carry on the vast multitude of lesser undertakings which associations daily enable American citizens to control? . . . The more government takes the place of associations, the more will individuals lose the idea of forming associations and need the government to come to their help. That is a vicious circle of cause and effect. . . . The morals and intelligence of a democratic people would be in as much danger as its commerce and industry if ever a government wholly usurped the place of private associations. Feelings and ideas are renewed, the heart enlarged, and the understanding developed only by the reciprocal action of men one upon another.

With this vicious circle in operation, the individual is left to stand bare and alone before the power of the state. A weak civil society requires more rules, regulations, and coercion. And in this circumstance citizens cannot help but feel isolated, defenseless, and dependent. In this way, Tocqueville said, government can "degrade men without tormenting them."

Before I leave the topic of government, I want to add one more observation. The expanding activities of government have also, in my experience, changed the nature of political involvement. More and more government actions involve the distribution of benefits to small groups of citizens, turning political debates into arguments over private spoils, not discussions of the public interest. It creates an atmosphere of shouting and suing, not deliberating, a political world of lobbyists and mailing lists and talk radio, inciting people to demand their rights and benefits. We have seen a rise in this kind of political activity, but it is not a sign of social health because it has no connection to the common good. It is the triumph of selfishness, not the practice of political community. And it demonstrates how government can warp the idea of citizenship, turning it into what has been called a "citizenship of disgruntled claimants."

A Free Market

Government is the first powerful force that has complicated the essential work of civic education. The second cursed blessing is harder for a conservative to discuss but still necessary. Many Americans, particularly American families, find that the most disruptive force in their moral lives is *not* government. It is a pervasive market that aggressively sells an ideology of consumption, immediate gratification, sexual freedom, and resentment of authority. They find more to fear from Madonna and the moral anarchy of the Internet than from Model Cities and the Great Society.

Once again, we cannot downplay the accomplishments of free markets that are the wonder of the age. They are history's most powerful tool to eliminate poverty, defeat disease, and extend life. And they make a moral contribution to every society that embraces them, justly rewarding risk, creativity, energy, and merit. But we also cannot downplay how markets can undermine the traditional institutions conservatives want to conserve. I have spent a considerable part of this past year on two issues: the Internet and the content rating of television programs. In both cases we are dealing with particularly pure free markets. Television programming depends directly on viewer demand. It embodies democracy. But much of what we get is vacuous or violent. As George Gilder observes, "Under the sway of television, democratic capitalism enshrines Gresham's law: bad culture drives out good, and ultimately porn and prurience, violence and blasphemy prevail everywhere from the dimwitted 'news' shows to the lugubrious movies."

The Internet, because it is anonymous, may be the purest market ever devised. Individuals are free to get precisely what they want at any given moment. And what that market produces, along with useful information, is a carnival of corruption—a world of pornography more extensive and depraved than you can imagine.

Conservatives must understand what most parents know by hard experience: Markets both respond to appetites and incite them, because it is possible to make a considerable amount of money feeding the weakness of human character. This is true of movie companies that assault taboo after taboo in a never ending race with boredom. It is true of entertainment companies that increase their market share with lyrics about the murder of policemen and the dismemberment of women. It is true of companies that market malt liquor, with its high alcohol content, specifically to inner-city communities. It is true of publicly traded companies that accumulate profit through the astounding proliferation of gaming, drawing income and savings from many who can least afford it. And all this is causing a backlash in America. From the Disney boycott to Bill Bennett's pop culture campaign, to the movement for television ratings, to legislative activity against indecency on the Internet, to the fight against legalized gambling—all these movements are directed toward limiting the destructive impact of markets, not government. And much of this activity is on the promarket right.

Markets are the cause of the wealth of nations. Yet conservatives would be wise to listen to advice from, of all people, John Maynard Keynes, written to his grandchildren in 1930: "But chiefly, do not let us overestimate the importance of the economic problem, or sacrifice to its supposed necessities other matters of greater significance. . . . The permanent problem of mankind is learning not just to live, but to live well."

A Higher Meaning

Americans committed to traditional moral and civic education have found it undermined by both government and markets. So the partisans of government and the partisans of markets, who dominate our political parties, seem irrelevant to our most urgent social problems and tasks. In fact, liberalism—both market liberalism and statist liberalism—misinterprets citizens' hopes and needs, which are higher than empty, procedural freedom and deeper than autonomy, choice, and consumption. According to Roger Scruton,

> There arises a longing for a value higher than the free pursuit of options and for a meaning greater than the protected privacy of the suburban living room or bedroom. All of a sudden, people wake up to the fact that the world has lost its sense, that they live in a society so atomized that there is no real reason—no reason that carries the endorsement of other people—for pursuing any of the infinite available options. And from this realization springs the longing for a community that will once again surround and embrace the individual and provide him with a goal that is greater than his own self-interest.

As a result of abandoning the founders' ideology, we have seen the return of the founders' fears—that we may be losing the moral order that makes it possible to be a liberal society. Freedom must be something more than promises we do not keep and oaths that never bind us. A wealthy nation can still display a poverty of purpose. And eventually there comes an understanding—a wisdom won from pain—that liberty unconstrained by character can destroy freedom. There comes a feeling that we have neglected the virtues on which republican order depends. There comes a recognition that self-government is crippled without self-control and that democracy depends on sources of legitimacy it does not create. "Men will more and more realize," wrote G. K. Chesterton, "that there is no meaning in democracy if there is no meaning in anything; and that there is no meaning in anything if the universe has not a center of significance and authority that is the author of our rights."

Virtue and Freedom

★

I want to return to the question posed at the outset: How do we encourage the virtue of a free nation and still leave it free? How do we reinforce or rebuild the moral infrastructure of freedom?

In this task we must understand that not all of civil society is created equal. The success of voluntary associations in creating civic virtue depends directly on the health of two institutions that cannot be called voluntary, at least not in the same way the Elks or bowling leagues can be called voluntary. These are the family and religion. The family to initiate us into the traditions of the human race—loyalty and love, diligence and duty. Religious institutions to instruct us in the spiritual purposes that make a good life possible, causing us, in Tocqueville's words, to sacrifice "a thousand ephemeral pleasures" in pursuit of "lasting happiness." He goes on to say, "Religious nations are naturally strong on the very points on which democratic nations are most weak; which shows of what importance it is for men to preserve their religion as their condition becomes more equal."

The renewal of liberal democracy will depend first and foremost on the strength of families, churches, and synagogues, which create citizens with the moral tools to cooperate in the common good. Pope John Paul II has stated,

"Solving serious national and international problems is not just a matter of economic production or of juridical or social organization, but calls for ethical and religious values. There is hope that the many people who profess no religion will also contribute to providing the necessary ethical foundation. But the Christian churches and the world religions will have a preeminent role in building a society worthy of man."

Upholding Morality

We need to understand that in a liberal society that elevates individual rights, it takes effort to maintain family and religion. Democracy, as Tocqueville predicted, can stamp its image on the institutions of civil society as individualism conquers the heart. Liberalism has a tendency to extend its assumptions to every area of life, dissolving bonds of duty and obligation. Professor James Q. Wilson writes the following about the modern family:

> Our popular culture, having spent years disassembling the family as a sociological institution, is now trying to reconstitute it as a purely voluntary association based on personal feelings. But the family in real life is based on impersonal feelings. We do not honor our father and mother because of the kinds of persons they are, but because they are our mother and father. We do not recognize their authority because they, in any sense, "deserve" it. We do so—and are pleased to do so—out of a natural sense of piety toward the authors of our being.

The same democratic tendency can be traced in religion when the search for self-fulfillment and self-esteem replaces submission to God's will.

All around us we see attempts to reinterpret or reinvent traditional institutions, stripping them of their moral demands, making them more acceptable to democratic men and women. But those moral demands are the essence of faith and family. And there is nothing more likely to destroy those institutions than the application of democracy to morality. We have all heard the refrains of modern political discussion: "Who are you to determine what a family is?" and "No one should judge anyone else"—arguments that reduce convictions to tastes. But holding together the commitments of a family, and serving the poor, and restraining our interests for the interests of others—these are difficult moral tasks, particularly in an age of relativism and self-interest. And people will only undertake those tasks if they believe with all their heart and mind that these tasks are good, noble, and virtuous—not just choices but immutable truths and moral laws and religious callings. We cannot remove these moral imperatives from families and churches and expect them to perform their social function. We believe in democracy because it is better to count heads than to break them. But we must reject a democracy of values in which every belief is equally true, equally false, and equally meaningless. The rejection of subjectivism is the precondition for a working civil society. So this is the first requirement of nurturing virtue in our culture: defending the existence of virtue itself, celebrating it in our families and churches.

The Role of Government

Defending virtue is the subject for another whole lecture. I want to focus on something more mundane and closer to my expertise. I want to end these remarks by talking about the role of government in fostering the virtues necessary to freedom. I have already detailed how a grasping, intrusive government can undercut democratic competence and disrupt civil society. But this should not lead to the simplistic belief that cutting or eliminating government is sufficient to rebuild civil society. In at least three ways the activities of government are essential to the health of associations and the cultivation of democratic virtue.

1. Govern Effectively

Effective government is often the prerequisite of a healthy civil society. Civic engagement is improbable when front porches attract random gunfire; when public meeting places become needle parks; when evening church services are canceled because reaching them is too dangerous. Escaping from poverty is more difficult when government discourages, through inverted incentives, the very traits of character that allow individuals to escape poverty. The value and importance of government has been tested and proven in two great, recent victories in the realm of social policy: welfare and crime.

When welfare reform was passed, critics predicted a million more children pushed into poverty and eleven million disadvantaged families shoved into suffering. What has happened could not be more different or more encouraging. In one year nationwide welfare caseloads have dropped by 18 percent—falling in every state except Hawaii. Six hundred and fifty thousand people left welfare in the four months after we passed the reform. Wisconsin—where welfare reform is far advanced—reduced those on welfare by 33 percent in one year. Since 1994 welfare rolls have fallen 48 percent in Oregon, 47 percent in Indiana, and 37 percent in Massachusetts.

The best and most recent analysis of these statistics tells a remarkable story. About one-third of the decline in the welfare rolls is because of economic growth. A national unemployment rate of 4.9 percent has allowed many to escape the trap of welfare. But about two-thirds of the recent decline is the result of a changed welfare culture. Faced with real time limits and real work requirements, many of the able-bodied have simply removed themselves from the welfare rolls. The results are even more impressive when one considers that they have not been accompanied by horror stories of soup lines, overburdened homeless shelters, and rising demand for other forms of alternative public assistance. In fact, welfare rolls declined at the same time as the rates of general poverty and child poverty fell.

Crime is another area in which effective government has proven its value. For a generation we were confidently told by experts that criminal behavior was rooted in hopeless, endless causes. Then William Bratton became head of New York's Metropolitan Transit Authority in 1990. He banned panhandling, removed graffiti, and arrested fare beaters, many of whom turned out to have weapons. The felony rate in the subway fell by 75 percent, a result that has been called "unprecedented" in the literature of criminology. Then Bratton took over the New York City Police Department in 1994, applying the same principles and attacking disorderly behavior, aggressive panhandlers, and squeegee men. By the end of 1995 residents of New York were less likely to be robbed or murdered than at any time in twenty-five years.

Effective government assures citizens that their communities are not beyond control and that they are not alone in defending civilized standards. When government does not maintain order or winks at destructive behavior, it communicates a form of social acceptance or social indifference. So by the mere act of defending and enforcing high standards, government can strengthen those who obey and uphold them, making law-abiding citizens feel less lonely, isolated, and besieged.

2. Create a Moral Atmosphere

The law plays an essential role in defining and defending the moral standards of a community. It cannot impose virtue, but it can help create an atmosphere in which civic institutions can do their work. That atmosphere is fostered when local communities restrict the zoning of pornographic bookstores and liquor stores and prosecute prostitution; when states reform divorce laws to favor the interests of children; when the federal government favors families and charities in the tax code and fights the importation of drugs. The federal role in these efforts is limited because it takes local communities to enforce community standards. Yet at whatever level, the law has an important role to play. When it comes to the decency of public culture, the moral atmosphere in which children are raised, or the stability of the family, government "neutrality" is indistinguishable from surrender.

It is a common argument, when it comes to indecency, that adults have a right to see whatever they want. "If you don't like it, don't buy it, or change the channel." But every citizen is affected by those who do not change the channel and those who insist on buying degraded and degrading material. Every citizen is forced to live in a coarsened society desensitized to violence and inundated with sex, a society that assaults the innocence of children and complicates their moral education. Michael Medved argues, "To say that if you don't like the popular culture then turn it off, is like saying, if you don't like smog, stop breathing. . . . There are Amish kids in Pennsylvania who know about Madonna."

Civil libertarians, who cannot reasonably deny that indecency is pervasive, are forced to argue that it is unimportant, that children are not really influenced by what they see and hear, that images and lyrics of casual sex and mindless violence have no relation to the prevalence of casual sex and mindless violence. But this argument proves too much. "After all," says Irving Kristol, "if you believe that no one was ever corrupted by a book, you also have to believe that no one was ever improved by a book (or a play or a movie). You have to believe, in other words, that all art is morally trivial and that, consequently, all education is morally irrelevant. No one . . . really believes that."

When government pretends to be indifferent to the moral character of society, it exercises a moral influence of its own. If it is forbidden to say that pornography or gambling is bad for the character or that divorce and illegitimacy violate moral duties and hurt children, it says that these things are permissible, because law will always be a moral teacher. And it can teach low standards as well as high. In the liberal view laws must be morally neutral, because we cannot know what is good. But because we cannot know what is good, there is no other commonly accepted social standard but the law. So laws become the only objective standard of conduct in society, and a low standard at that. By refusing to recognize the moral ideals of its people, the liberal state actually undermines those ideals.

3. Support Civic Institutions

Government plays a role in strengthening the compassionate work of private and religious institutions in communities in which the scale of those efforts is not sufficient to the need. It is true that an overly centralized, regulatory, and litigious state has "crowded out" civil society in many ways. But it is wrong to expect that the retreat of government will automatically result in a rebirth of broken families and decimated communities. Relimiting government is a necessary but not sufficient condition for a strong civil society. Conservatives, concerned with practical realities and familiar with the law of unintended consequences, must consider an additional point. Princeton professor John DiIulio Jr. uses this example: If a victim is stabbed, you need to pull out the knife. But pulling out the knife alone will not heal the person. Getting government out of our lives will not *ipso facto* lead to a rebirth of community institutions and republican virtue.

In Russia, for example, as government retreated we saw the emergence of what one observer called "anarcho-capitalism," something closer to the Mafia than to the invisible hand. Even if the result had been known beforehand, it would not have been an argument for retaining the communist system. But it is an argument for respecting the potential for social dislocation when civil society is weak. We should not ignore the potential for suffering, especially in our cities, as government withdraws. The state cannot directly rebuild civic institutions. Yet particularly in some communities, we must find ways to encourage these institutions to renew themselves. The alternative is a destructive indifference to human suffering, a kind of social Darwinism by default.

The Project for American Renewal

The rebuilding of civil society has been my struggle in the last few years as I have tried to translate some of these ideas into legislation. The result is the Project for American Renewal. It is not a government plan to rebuild the civic sector—a self-contradictory idea. It attempts instead to take the side of people and institutions who are rebuilding their own communities and who often feel isolated, poorly funded, and poorly equipped. Its components direct attention and resources to community development corporations, religious charities, private schools for inner-city children, neighborhood watches, and communities trying to restore the legal importance of marriage and family. The goal, whenever possible, is to apply private resources of compassion and moral instruction to public problems, expanding the society while limiting the state.

The centerpiece of the plan is a charity tax credit. It would allow every taxpaying family to give one thousand dollars of what it owes the government each year to a private charity in their community. It is my expectation that most people would prefer giving to the Salvation Army instead of to the Department of Health and Human Services, to Habitat for Humanity instead of to the Department of Housing and Urban Development. I am convinced that in welfare policy, devolution and block grants are simply not enough. It is not sufficient to shift programs from federal bureaucrats to state bureaucrats, who often have the same blind spots and limitations. It is my belief that a bold new agenda of public compassion should adopt this bold objective: to break the monopoly of government as a provider of compassion and return its resources to individuals, churches, and charities. I have tried to define an approach guided by a simple principle: In circumstances when government must act, it should always act in ways that strengthen, not undermine, the web of institutions that create community.

Subsidiarity and Sphere Sovereignty

This approach, I believe and hope, is consistent with a great and noble tradition of Catholic and Protestant social thought originating before the turn of the century with Pope Leo XIII and Abraham Kuyper. The parallel teachings of subsidiarity and sphere sovereignty have enriched our political debates with some basic principles.

1. There is a common good greater than individual rights, and society must actively and tirelessly seek it. Kuyper exclaimed, "We shall not be satisfied with the structure of society until it offers all human beings an existence worthy of man." In a beautiful passage Pope John XXIII defines the common good as "the sum total of those conditions of social living, whereby men are enabled more fully and more readily to achieve their own perfections."

2. Though society must seek the common good, society is not identical with the state. A healthy society, in fact, is composed of countless institutions that are not expressions of either politics or the market. These include churches, schools, unions, fraternal groups, neighborhood associations, and other mediating structures. "State and society," said Kuyper, "each has its own sphere, its own sovereignty, and so one should not try to absorb the other." Pope John Paul II has written, "A community of a higher order should not interfere in the internal life of a community of a lower order. . . . In fact, it would appear that needs are best understood and satisfied by people who are closest to them and who act as neighbors to those in need."

3. A good, rough definition of social justice is the flourishing of these institutions—protected from both market individualism and intrusive government. The Catechism describes the proper role of the state as being "to defend and promote the common good of civil society, its citizens and intermediary bodies." Pope John XXIII stated, "There is always wide scope for humane action by private citizens and for Christian charity. . . . It is evident that in stimulating efforts relating to spiritual welfare, the work done by individual men and by private civic groups has more value than what is done by public authorities."

I think this goal—"stimulating efforts relating to spiritual welfare"—is causing the most exciting, important debates in social policy. It is an objective that allows us to emphasize the civilizing, humanizing role of religion and morality in our social order without violating our commitment to pluralism. Many of our worst social problems will only yield to moral solutions: the renewal of parental commitment to children, the internal restraint of impulsive violence and aggressive sexuality, the return of public spirit and civic engagement. Mediating institutions teach these lessons. By supporting them broadly, government can promote moral answers to human problems without favoring or sponsoring any one moral or religious vision. The principles of subsidiarity and sphere sovereignty thus give us an insight into how government can encourage the virtue of a free nation and still leave it free, by encouraging the work of civil society without overwhelming it with rules and restrictions.

Conclusion

In 1783 George Washington, the symbol of republican virtue, wrote to a friend, "We are a young nation and have a character to establish. . . . This is the time of our political probation . . . the moment to establish or ruin our national character forever." In the view of the founders our national character would directly determine the future of freedom, though they feared freedom might sap our strength of character. It is civil society that stands between those fears and their realization—that teaches the moral prerequisites for democracy and leavens liberty with law.

In a democracy our probation is permanent, because every generation is a new nation, to be taught the habits of heart and mind that permit representative government. So we as a nation need to understand and embrace the paradox that our liberal goals depend on the existence of moral truth and the health of institutions that nurture it. We need to understand that freedom depends on a culture worthy of freedom. And we need to understand that now, and at every time, we are a young nation with a character to establish.

The Limits of Policy Reform

Response by Glenn C. Loury

It is an honor to offer a response to Senator Coats's provocative and important statement on the relationship between justice and morality—between government and society. Let me begin with a brief personal declaration about how I approach the task at hand.

Professionally I am an academic economist. My scholarly work involves the study of markets and business firms, the analysis of buying low and selling high, of maximizing behavior, rational choice, and the like. I believe this to be important work. We must be mindful of the incentives created by social programs, of the costs and benefits involved in government regulations, and of the technical difficulties associated with the accurate measurement of these costs and benefits.

Yet spiritually speaking, I am a Christian. As a believer I do not find the analytical perspective by itself adequate to the task of social prescription. Indeed, I sometimes find a

Glenn C. Loury is professor of economics and director of the Institute on Race and Social Division at Boston University. He is an essayist, social critic, and lecturer. His book *One by One, from the Inside Out: Essays and Reviews on Race and Responsibility in America* (New York: Free Press, 1995) won the 1996 American Book Award and the 1996 Christianity Today Book Award.

single-minded focus on benefits and costs to be a profoundly impoverished way of thinking about how we should live together in society.

I recently wrote, regarding a particular work of social science, that after reading the book, I was even more impressed with the limited utility of the social sciences in the management of human affairs. What I meant was that social science sees only a part of the human subject as the venue of its study. Our methods reduce the entirety of the person to the materialistic and deterministic dimension that we think we understand. In so doing, the social scientist leaves out that which most makes a person human; we leave out the soul. It is my fundamental conviction that human beings are not defined by our desires at a point in time; I would claim that we are not even defined by our biological inheritances. As I wrote in that article, God is not finished with us when he deals us our genetic hand. As spiritual beings, what we are in the fullness of our humanity transcends that which can be grasped with the particular vision that an economist, sociologist, or psychologist brings.

I want to emphasize that I am not here repudiating the life of the intellect. I am simply saying that to grasp fully the nature of the human subject, intellectuals must reckon with this transcendent dimension. I am arguing against arrogance in the academy, not against the use of our intellects. What I reject is the presumption that intellect on its own can do for us what it plainly cannot do—tell us the meaning of our lives. Social science cannot finally resolve the most profound questions at the center of our struggles as individuals, as families, and as a nation. Who are we? What must we do? How shall we live? What is right? When all the statistical analyses have been rendered, we still have to step back and ask questions such as these. Absent the spiritual grounding that permits such questions to be meaningfully posed, the rest of our intellectual efforts amount to so much puzzle solving that in the end has no life. It is in this spirit that I approach the discussion of the matters before us.

The Fruit of Modernity

The central paradox with which Senator Coats is concerned may be described as follows: America, a liberal country, relies on the vitality of conservative institutions to maintain among the citizenry the habits of moral character on which the success of democracy depends. I agree with this point and with the importance Senator Coats attaches to it. The senator quotes disapprovingly from the Supreme Court's *Casey* decision, in which the majority declared in support of abortion rights that at the heart of liberty lies the freedom for individuals to define their own meaning of the cosmos. He intends with this quote to call to our attention the evils of materialism and relativism and the threat of the extreme individualism that now infects our most august and important public institutions.

I agree with and am concerned about all of this. But just what is to be done? I must point out that these phenomena are the fruit of a modernity that is upon us and that will not be rolled back by any of the instruments of public policy mentioned by the senator. Tremendous forces of social change are remaking our world. Consider the movement called feminism. Who remains now to openly challenge the necessity of the liberation of women? Who can deny the profound import of the restructuring of family relationships, of the sexual liberation, of the erosion of consensus attitudes and broadly acknowledged taboos about sexuality, which has occurred in the past half century? Is it not fantasy to suppose that the old ways of life will be reestablished?

I fear that Senator Coats underestimates the depth of the difficulty associated with the passing away of old restraints and with the erosion of conservative institutions. These are features of late modernity not just in America but in all economically advanced societies. Divorce rates have soared; out-of-wedlock birthrates have risen sharply; sexual mores have been dramatically rewritten; relativistic beliefs are rampant. Consider that all the major religious institutions are themselves under the sway of these forces of modernism, relativism, and individualism. This is true not only of the mainline Protestant denominations but even in the evangelical community, in the Catholic church, and within Judaism. The influences of modernity are at work; the old verities are under attack. The moral dictates of our forebears' traditions are under unrelenting pressure; they are being rethought and redefined even as we speak. How shall we respond to these developments while pursuing justice and strengthening our democratic institutions? I fear that the senator offers us little guidance on this question.

The Limits of Public Policy

There is a fundamental distinction to be drawn here between the role of government, politics, and public policy on the one hand and the role of prophetic witness, spiritual revival, and the building of new, energetic, and vital religious community on the other. The senator's focus is on the former role, but my view is that only the latter role offers real hope of preserving the moral foundation upon which the success of our democracy depends.

Through government, politics, and policy we can fashion laws that signal our moral commitments against drugs, pornography, or premarital sex. This is not an insignificant thing. We can funnel resources into mediating, private institutions through tax incentives for charitable giving, for example. This can be helpful. And we can engage in paternalistic, coercive interventions in individuals' lives—through the administration of various government programs. There is a place for this. But at the end of the day these activities are insufficient to the restorative task at hand.

The reach of these policies is limited, and there can be negative repercussions from all of these undertakings. The signaling of values through law, in the face of widespread behavior contradicting the values in question, breeds cynicism and undermines the authority of the law. The fiasco of Prohibition surely taught us that. Expanding the charitable activities of private institutions through the massive infusion of public or tax-deductible funds runs the risk of changing the essence of those institutions, of attracting a different breed of person to work in them, and of distorting their missions. Finally, state-sanctioned coercion is a crude tool. One has only to consider the largest such undertaking, the prison system—populated by a million and a half American souls on a given day—to see how limited is the potential for getting where we really want to be by this route.

The senator is worried about the family. Looking across the globe, in Britain, France, Germany, Australia, Canada—indeed, in all of the OECD countries except Switzerland and Japan—illegitimacy rates are approximately five times higher today than they were in 1960. Divorce can be a terrible, tragic thing, particularly for children; there is no doubt. Yet consider that even within families that remain intact, the valuation of children as reflected in the time that parents are making available to their upbringing has dropped dramatically because of the deep cultural forces at work. A great many more families send both parents into the workforce now than ever before. And there is abroad in the land an ethos in which adults are more reluctant to sacrifice their personal fulfillment in order to promote a child's development. This, I suggest, is the real threat. The rise in divorce is but the effect of this deeper and more profound cause. How are we to fight it? Surely, putting more hurdles between divorcing parents and the courthouse is no solution.

The senator laments the extent of abortion in the land. Though I am no constitutional lawyer, I agree that *Roe v. Wade* should be overturned. Yet what could we expect to emerge from the political process in the states were they given the ability to legislate on abortion? It is improbable that this practice would be universally outlawed. A more likely outcome is that in many jurisdictions legal abortions would continue to be available. When Mother Teresa said of abortion, "My God, what kind of world have we come to where a baby is not safe from its own mother?" she was putting her finger on the heart of the matter.

Although Senator Coats does not mention the issue, it is instructive in this context to consider the debate over the morality of homosexuality. The normalization of this "lifestyle" is now well advanced. Again, though I am no constitutional lawyer, I found Justice Scalia's dissent more persuasive than Justice Kennedy's majority opinion in a recent case that overturned a Colorado ballot initiative limiting the enactment of homosexual rights legislation. Yet as I search the social landscape, I see the ability to make public arguments against "the abomination of homosexuality" slipping away like sand through one's fingers. This is not a moral issue usefully approached through the law. Even though the Court in *Bowers v. Hardwick* has held antisodomy laws to be constitutional, we know that such laws are not going to be enforced, given the current social ethos.

Thus, I see deep problems with this tendency to turn to the law as an instrument for fending off the corrosive effects of modernity. It works poorly for many problems. And for others it works too well in that we fail to mobilize for spiritual warfare because we think we can legislate evil out of existence. ("Our struggle is not against flesh and blood, but against the rulers, . . . authorities, . . . powers . . ., and against the spiritual forces of evil" [Eph. 6:12]). And there is the problem of pluralism. Not every conception of good is universally shared in the polity, nor should every conception of good be given the force of law, even when we have the votes. Finally, there is the danger of self-righteousness and hypocrisy. "Moral scolding" through public policy can become a seductive activity that deflects us from detecting the mote in our own eye.

I spent some time this summer reading Leo Tolstoy's nonfiction writings. He became an eccentric pacifist and radical Christian critic at the end of his life. And I was stunned at the force of some of his arguments. (Although I must say I was not entirely persuaded, particularly on his point that a true Christian must be celibate!) He argues quite provocatively that the core of Christianity lies in the Sermon on the Mount. You see this fellow committing adultery? Well, have you lusted in your own heart? This is a teaching quite relevant to our contemporary public scene. The point is that while the behavioral pathologies and cultural threats we see in society—the moral erosions "out there"—are bad, nevertheless our crusade against them can take on a pathological dimension of its own. We can become self-righteous, legalistic, ungenerous, stiff-necked, and hypocritical. We become unable to see the mote in our own eye. We neglect to raise questions of social justice. We fail to ask how, for example, the moral decay and behavioral pathology of the underclass is related to systemic factors—our economy driven by private gain, our culture of endemic materialism, and our vacuous political discourses. Perhaps the problems of the underclass are but the excreta at the bottom end of the social spectrum of a much more profound and widespread moral deviance.

Reweaving the Social Fabric

The magnitude of the dilemma here is enormous once we accept that there are no quick fixes, that the old norms may never be reestablished. It is not possible, when 70 percent of the people in a given community are doing something, to have that thing be broadly understood as a terrible evil within that community. We have to face the fact that one cannot push on a string. Without doubt the effect of modernity—in regard to sexuality and adult responsibility to the home, for example—has been to pull on the loose thread of the social fabric, thus unraveling it. However, this does not mean that by fighting against the effect of modernity through legislation and moral suasion—by in effect pushing on the loose thread—we can somehow reweave the garment. It may be that we have to create new institutions, that we have to come up with different conceptions of how to live our lives together in the face of these modernistic forces.

When there is an unraveling of the moral fabric, it is necessary to ask who has the authority to reconstruct it. And what is the source of that authority? In my view there is something about human relationships that is essential to the establishment of this authority. Consequently, the building of authoritative and respectful relationships where they do not now exist becomes a principal requirement if we are to be serious about forestalling the destructive effect of modernity.

This point is of special importance when thinking about the moral breakdown in the inner city. The fundamental thing that needs to be established, and is not yet established in American public discourse about the problems of the inner city, is that we are all in this together. Those people are our people, whether they be black or white, crack-addicted or juvenile felons, or worse. And speaking as a Christian, the imperative is love. "God did not send his Son into the world to condemn the world, but to save the world through him" (John 3:17). I cry out as a Christian with the desire to see in the public political witness of the activist Christian community more of a reflection of that compassionate posture. Now, I recognize that there are problems here of implementation, of how compassion manifests itself and of the ways in which it can go wrong. But I can distinguish those problems of implementation from the spirit that I think ought to animate our participation in public and political life with regard to these issues. It should be a spirit of charity and a spirit of love.

There are chasms separating us that we should work to bridge—chasms of race and class. I would argue that different elements of the Christian community are prevented by such chasms from being in the kind of relationship with one another out of which genuine compassion can be realized. I believe that the links between inner-city and suburban, black and white, poor and middle-class Christian communities should be stronger than they are. There is work of connection and reconciliation that needs doing here. I wish that Senator Coats, in his discussions of justice and civil society, had said more about this aspect of the problem.

Additional Reservations

In conclusion, I want to state clearly that I am sympathetic to what Senator Coats hopes to achieve with his Project for American Renewal—the strengthening of civil society and the devolution of responsibilities for social reconstruction from government into the voluntary sector. But the scope and scale of the requisite change makes me nervous. And I must also point out that his approach is ideological. I mean that as a description, not an evaluation. A core set of political beliefs animates the effort: government in Washington has grown too big; we have an opportunity to reverse the historic dynamic. There is a certain revolutionary zeal involved. Nobody knows what, exactly, will come in its train.

My conservative disposition makes me cautious about taking a set of simple ideas and using them to restructure a vast social undertaking. Such caution is a reflection of prudence—a high conservative virtue. Millions of Americans now depend on a welfare-state apparatus that, however flawed, also has some great achievements (Medicare and

Social Security) to its credit. I do not believe dismantling the Department of Health and Human Services or eliminating food stamps, Medicaid, and housing assistance to the poor are appropriate goals for federal policy at this time. I would not quickly change the conditions under which so many people depend for their support, without having a pretty clear idea about what I expected to happen as a consequence of doing so.

Finally, I am also ambivalent about a vision that sees the churches as primary instruments of social-service provision. If you were to ask me what churches should do, I would say, "The church should first and foremost be the church." It should be about spiritual business. If it were, the people would go out into the world and do what needs doing. The government bureaucrat, the university professor, the businessperson, and the lawyer all would be more Christlike in the administration of their affairs. The church should not be seen primarily as an institution through which programs are administered. I am loath to think about churches as vehicles for funneling scores of billions of dollars into the hands of needy people. The fundamental spiritual mission of the church, if carried out successfully, could create throughout society ripple effects of far greater influence than any works that could possibly be carried out within the institutional setting of the churches themselves.

Fighting Poverty
for the Common Good

Response by Mary Nelson

I come to this discussion of civil society and the role of government from "outside the box." My world on the west side of Chicago is so different: an African-American community in which 40 percent of the people live on incomes below the poverty line and half of them are working poor; in which the basic systems of society, including the school system, the justice system, the police system, the transit system, the financial system, and government, generally do not work well. So I have a jaundiced view. Yet it is in the struggle for jobs and opportunity, in the struggle for better living conditions and safe streets, that we have found the fullest sense of community—of civil society. From this vantage point I want to respond to the senator's remarks and then share a few comments of my own.

Mary Nelson is founder and president of Bethel New Life, a nationally recognized Christian community development organization in Chicago. She manages more than four hundred employees and a seven million dollar budget to provide affordable housing, job training, health and family services, education, and community empowerment. Her awards include honorary doctoral degrees and the 1993 Raoul Wallenberg Humanitarian Award.

55

Experiencing Community

It took some exploration on my part to think through what this civil society business is all about. Between the prince (government wielding the authority of the law) and the merchant (marketplace driven by the imperatives of self-interest) stand both the individual and associations (civil society). There is a constant tension between individual self-interest and the civil society's common good. My experience of civil society is in church groups, clubs, community development corporations (such as the one I am part of), and civic groups functioning in between government, the corporate community, and the individual. Civil society must include some experience of the common good.

When I was founding principal of a high school for dropouts, we started the school with only one rule: "Your freedom ends where the next person's freedom begins." The experience of being annoyed by someone chewing gum loudly or playing disturbing music provided the occasion to talk about the trade-offs between individual freedom and the common good. Many years later in my community development work, we were developing a sweat equity housing co-op, and the families were quarreling about who would get which apartment: "I got here first, so I should get the apartment I want"; "I've done more sweat work, so I should get the best apartment." One night after a lot of this discussion, someone shared the idea of identifying apartments based on individual family situations (such as a three-bedroom apartment for the family with the most kids). Community then became a reality.

Poverty is now much more concentrated in our country, and we have more to worry about with the lack of experience of community that crosses class and color lines. Robert Reich, former secretary of labor, wrote a telling article several years ago titled "The Secession of the Successful," in which he lamented the decrease in citizen support for formerly basic community institutions such as libraries, public mass transportation, police, and public schools. The wealthy, he pointed out, were creating their own gated communities with security systems and private police, using internets instead of libraries, sending their children to privileged private schools, and using superhighways for their cars. They no longer had much need for the public institutions and thus were not supporting bond issues and legislation that kept these systems fully functional.

Teaching Cooperation

Senator Coats asks who is teaching our children the values of democracy and the common good, and suggests that it is the responsibility of families and religion. It seems to me we used to think public education was the institution for teaching civics and democracy. No more. We thought public education could be value-neutral, yet it taught competition, not cooperation. It operated on a totalitarian model of conduct even while trying to teach participatory democracy. However, there is hope. Many schools now have students involved in team projects, service learning, and more.

A concerned priest in Mondragon, Spain, many years ago started a technical training school to help unemployed young men. It was organized around participatory (democratic) governance and decision making, with the youth as participants. When these young men went off into technical factory jobs, they soon became frustrated that their ideas and energy were not appreciated in the factory setting. After a few years, with the priest's help, they began worker-owned industrial cooperatives. Now Mondragon cooperatives have over twelve thousand employees and own and operate banks, food stores, and the largest home appliance manufacturers in Europe. Mondragon annually trains the worker-owners in the co-op principles and skills of governance.

We, by contrast, have allowed the public school system to become a system of savage inequality, not a melting pot, stepping-stone to equal opportunity, or trainer in democracy and experience of pluralism for our youth. Jonathan Kozol, in his book *Savage Inequality*, details the perpetuation of this inequality in the property-tax-based funding of public schools and the often second-rate and lackluster education that most ghetto youth get. No wonder they cannot find jobs in today's workplace.

Achieving Success?

Senator Coats gives several examples of government success in dealing with current issues. He claims that welfare reform is already a success, with an 18 percent decline in caseloads overall. Princeton University professor John DiIulio Jr., in an article in the *Weekly Standard* (October 20, 1997) titled "Welfare Reform as We Know It," says, "It is true that between March 1994 and May 1997 the AFDC rolls dropped by 23.3 percent—from 4.6 million households to 3.5 million households. But they had risen dramatically in the early 1990s, and the recent decline left nearly 33,000 more households on AFDC in May 1997 than in July 1989." Clearly, it is too early to tell.

More important, in shaping welfare reform, government lost focus on what should be the real aim—to overcome poverty. Again, in our community on Chicago's west side, 40 percent of the people are living on incomes below the poverty line, and half of them have low-wage jobs. Rebecca Blank, a Northwestern University professor, shares a startling fact in her book *It Takes a Nation*. The marketplace and a growth economy are no longer the major influence in moving people out of poverty. In 1993 the United States had economic growth of 3 percent, but at the same time the number of people living in poverty rose. "This is troubling," Blank says, "because of the long cherished belief that economic growth is the sure way to reduce need." This is caused by factors such as low-wage, low-skill jobs, the internationalization of labor, and technological advancements and skill requirements. Professor Blank goes on to say, "The most attractive goal for the U.S. antipoverty efforts is a policy to increase work and earnings among adults so they can escape poverty through their own earnings." Action includes a variety of steps to deal with welfare and poverty, such as the Earned Income Tax Credit and living-wage jobs.

To understand the vital role of government, it is important to include "liberty and justice for all." Ironically, the title of Senator Coats's paper is "Mending Fences: Renewing Justice between Government and Civil Society," but there has been little discussion of justice. Government has the mandate to ensure justice. When states had varying degrees of Jim Crow laws, it took a federal voting rights act and the civil rights legislation to bring about a modicum of justice for all citizens. When government sanctioned and ignored injustice, a meaningful democratic society was impossible.

In our Judeo-Christian tradition we are called to speak up, to risk the wrath of government in identifying injustice in the land. "Let justice roll down" is the battle cry when government and society have become out of balance. We, as Christians, need to be willing to stand against, to stand apart from, government or civil society when justice hangs in balance.

Promoting the Common Good

I now want to make a few comments on civil society.

1. We need a creative tension between government and civil society, a balance between the competing forces, to have a healthy society. At the Mondragon cooperatives they call it "equilebrio"—a balance between interests and needs, between technological imperatives and social objectives, between financial needs of the firm and economic needs of

members, between the individual good and the common
good of the community.

*2. We need to be clear about the most important value or
principle of our Judeo-Christian belief and of democracy—
the innate dignity and worth of every person in God's sight.*
Our founders were clear about this: "with liberty and justice
for all." If this is clear, it changes the way we look at things,
at the functions of government and the notion of the common good. I have been involved in a five-year-long process
to write a social statement on economic life for the Evangelical Lutheran Church in America. The committee, composed of business owners, workers, theologians, and community activists, held listening posts, read a lot, and heard
from many people. We have come to a guiding statement
around which to judge contemporary situations: The aim of
the economy should be a sufficient, sustainable livelihood
for all.

*3. We need to create new partnerships and collaborations—
between government and the marketplace, between government and citizens groups, churches, and individuals.* Government has a critical role to play, not as the only actor but
as participant and partner. There should be new alignments,
including regional approaches that unite things such as land
planning, public transportation, health care, taxation for education, and so forth.

*4. We need to place a higher value on the work of commu-
nity.* Why are child care workers, who teach our children in
their most impressionable years, so underpaid? Citizenship
is about public service, about claims we make on each other,
obligations we have to one another. Community is the place
in which we function as citizens. Senator Coats, in his *Project for American Renewal,* also suggests that we need to encourage and support community efforts: "Government

should actively but not intrusively assist grassroots activists and organizations rebuilding the social and moral infrastructure of their neighborhoods . . . community empowerment. The mediating structures are the principal expressions of the real values and the real needs of people in society. . . . Public policy should recognize, respect and where possible empower these institutions." The way to empower the citizenry is not through a therapeutic model or compassionate acts of individuals toward "the poor" but rather through engaged citizens who participate in the solutions and the action.

5. Finally, we need to be reminded of our common purpose, of God's vision for the human community. When going through a strategic planning process, participants must first collectively refine the mission statement, the purpose and values of an organization. Such a process at this time in our country could be unifying and energizing. Those of us who hold a Judeo-Christian faith hold in our hands the treasure of God's vision for the human community, of God's promise to be with the widows and orphans, of the demands of justice. This vision and purpose gives us the energy to seek justice in the land, to hold kings and governments under the judgment of God, and to experience in so doing a sense of community and of participatory democracy.

Toward a Christian Social Policy

Response by Stanley W. Carlson-Thies

Senator Coats gives a challenging analysis of what ails the American experiment, providing context and rationale for his Project for American Renewal, an innovative legislative response to some of our most troubling social problems. The lecture is the mature fruit of a significant career in public service. Yet the senator shows no hesitation in overriding the boundaries of the conventional political battle. His diagnosis and prescription reject not only the liberals' hope in governmentalism but also the libertarianism and market celebration currently dominant in his own circle of conservatives and Republicans. Senator Coats honors both government and civil society, for both of them are God-given institutional realms; indeed, the senator's desire is to bring them into proper relationship, to "renew justice" between them. His desire is to fulfill his legislative office as a Christian public servant.

Stanley W. Carlson-Thies is director of social policy studies at the Center for Public Justice and is the country's leading expert on the charitable choice provision of the 1996 federal welfare reform law. He is the director of several projects at the Center on welfare policies and is coeditor of and contributing author to *Welfare in America: Christian Perspectives on a Policy in Crisis* (Grand Rapids: Eerdmans, 1996).

63

He thereby honors the driving passion of Abraham Kuyper, whose most characteristic belief was the conviction that no part of creation stands outside Christ's rule of judgment and redemption. For Kuyper, Christian politics is a dynamic and creative effort that cannot be confined to the polarized options rooted in secular visions. And a particular concern must be the positive tasks, and not only the limits, of government. Senator Coats's paper has just these intentions. Yet I think we must ask whether the analysis is Christian enough and whether the policy alternative he offers sufficiently acknowledges the responsibility of government to do justice. The other respondents share my disquiet on these points.

A Christian Political Perspective

Senator Coats's public service is driven by his desire to bring justice to a broken world. America, this great and generous land, is afflicted by grievous ills that demand response. The poverty and social distress of our urban centers and of the so-called underclass are at the heart of his concern. But he points equally to dysfunction in the rest of society: rampant divorce, greed, self-centeredness, moral relativism. The founders of the American republic, he points out, worried that a nation dedicated to liberty and blessed with material success might not preserve a moral culture. It seems that their fears have come true. Rich materially, we are increasingly impoverished morally.

Worse, the senator argues, the social ills issue from the heart of the American experiment. The ills that beset us are the evil fruit of an overextension of the positive traits that generated our successes. Individual striving, a passion for choices, dissatisfaction with the status quo—such qualities undergird and fuel our democratic polity and market society. Taken to extremes, however, they undermine the social order and have spawned myriad social dysfunctions.

Liberty is the soul of democracy, for instance, but the refusal of adults to be bound spells death for families and distress for children. Both democracy and economy depend on each participant asserting self-interest; yet without an equal dedication to the common good, a social order cannot be sustained.

The founders had a solution. In their blueprint the drive for liberty and the striving for self-fulfillment were to be disciplined by the institutions of civil society and the virtues nurtured within them. Families not only provide our entry into society but shape us to civility. We form associations to advance our goals but are in turn formed by the institutions, which can exist only when we temper our self-interest to the joint effort and empathize with the interests and needs of those with whom we rub shoulders. The great paradox of America, Senator Coats points out, is that the viability of our great liberal public institutions is dependent on the vitality of the conservative institutions of private life.

Yet in our time many of these private institutions, rather than undergirding the public order, are themselves crumbling. The influence has flowed in the wrong direction: Civil society has been subverted by the very structures and forces it was intended to temper. Market passions and forces have unleashed boundless self-interest, destablizing social institutions. Most important, expanding government itself has undermined civil society, displacing citizens' efforts to help themselves and their neighbors, rewarding self-destructive behavior, and by emphasizing material benefits, converting political action from participation in establishing the common good into a battle for private advantage.

Thus, Senator Coats insists, beyond the incessant disputes about political issues both petty and momentous, international and domestic, the chief public policy question is this: whether and how government can be made to have a constructive, restorative role in society. How can government become a support for the social institutions so vital to the health of citizens and crucial to its own function and persistence? At the fundamental level the issue is this: How can government uphold conservative institutions and the moral values they embody, but in the American way—consonant with liberty?

In his analysis the senator makes little explicit mention of specifically Christian values. Nevertheless, his evangelical Christian standpoint is clear enough in the evaluative standards he employs, not only in his disapproval of abortion, homosexuality, and divorce but equally in his condemnation of materialism and unbounded individualism. However, what must strike us about his analysis is how much it is confined to the terms of the founding of America. We have departed from the fullness of the founders' design and thus are realizing the founders' fears, he argues. The solution must be to return to their design. A Christian evaluation may help us see the depths of our sins, but it is the founders' framework within which we must find our solutions. Or could it be that the senator wants to suggest that the founders' framework itself is a Christian framework?

This focus on the genius of the founders must be disquieting. As we experience the moral decline of our nation, recognize the persisting distress of many of our fellow citizens, and witness the unraveling of ties and institutions, should we not be driven to our knees to ask from whence cometh our salvation? And if we do so, must we expect to stay within the confines of America's founding? We are Christians, citizens of another and greater kingdom, and not only the temporary citizens of this political order. Why should we, then, take as our baseline commitment those values and practices that define our democracy and our liberal institutions?

Take specifically the matter of the constraints our system places on religion. We may well agree with the founders that the logic of their system requires government not to establish religion. Yet in our present time of peril why should Christians, concerned equally with how our young slip away from us thanks to commerce, the Internet, and the public schools as well as with the poverty and social decline of inner cities, not seek a full dose of religion for our culture, administered by infusing the true faith into our dominating institutions?

Indeed, as Glenn Loury suggests in his response, the collapse of our social and moral order is not likely the consequence simply of excessive and mistaken government programs and the destructive effects of the market. Postmodernism is the driving force, a philosophy—or rather religion—of its own, which moreover has infected even conservative Protestant communities. If so, do we not need a frontal, full-strength, religious battle instead of a return to the designs of the founders? They may have been content, as Senator Coats points out, with "citizens not of perfect Christian virtue but with democratic habits and manners," but do not our current crisis and our own convictions tell us that what we need is a purified Christian nation?

But in truth such a plea expresses a mistaken polarity, a dangerous misunderstanding of how the line between the kingdom of God and the kingdom of darkness intersects with the political and cultural battle lines of our nation. The ultimate battle is not in our hands; the final judgment is not ours to proclaim. Christian totalitarianism is a contradiction in terms, as the founders sensed. However, the essential point is just this: If Christian citizens are to accept the separation of church and state, it must be on Christian grounds, on the foundation of a biblical perspective on society and government, and not because of the logic or imperatives of the American experiment. For it is when we seek first the kingdom of the risen Lord that we can find *shalom* and the right ordering for earthly kingdoms, and not the other way around. The Bible, in fact, instructs us on the limits of government, the competencies of other social institutions, and the need for people willingly to be adopted into a renewed relationship with God. It is in such guidance, and not the blueprint of the founders, that we must finally find the justification for our political philosophy.

Particularly in this time of cultural decay and spiritual confusion and decline, it is imperative that we search for a firmer foundation than the American founding. Otherwise when the spiritual battle becomes intense, we will be driven either to deify this nation and its ideals or else, in the name of spiritual purity and vigor, to reject those "liberal" elements for which, rather, we should thank God.

The Justice Task of Government

What, then, should be our response to the crisis of the American experiment and the social ills afflicting our nation? Senator Coats insists that a key part of the solution is action by the federal government. He is not looking, of course, for a magical intervention from Washington that will heal the nation; in his conception the means of change, and also its goal, consists of the renewal of personal virtue and the revitalization of civil society. Government programs are no substitute for good action by citizens and the health of the nongovernment sphere. Yet, he insists, government has a positive contribution to make.

Here he parts company with the libertarians who have so strongly shaped the contemporary conservative debate about social policy. Although he agrees with them that federal programs have often made problems worse and that government action can crowd out responses by neighbors and associations, he rejects their conclusion that the key policy directive is for the federal government to stop intervening. This is social Darwinist advice, in the senator's view; it leaves the problems unaddressed and requires that government abdicate its task of ensuring justice to those who are crying out for help.

What is needed is a different kind of government action, action that builds up civil society and energizes civic activism. What government—even the federal government—can and must do is "take the side of people and institutions who are rebuilding their own communities and who often feel isolated, poorly funded, and poorly equipped." Government should use its authority and resources to empower citizens and their associations—the agents of lasting and positive change for distressed families and neighborhoods. Thus the centerpiece of Senator Coats's legislative package, the Project for American Renewal, is a charity tax credit by which government can stimulate citizens to give more generously to private and faith-based charities that serve the needy. In this way the federal government can become a positive force in civil society rather than a substitute for its institutions.

Senator Coats is right to see that the key social policy issue of our era is how to properly relate government to the nongovernment institutions of society. Although much debate in Washington and in state capitals throughout the nation remains a duel between pro- and anti-government partisans, the major political dynamic around the world is the realignment of government, nonprofit organizations, and market institutions. As Senator Coats and his colleagues in the congressional Renewal Alliance recognize, the answer to the unfulfilled promise of the welfare state is not merely to turn from government but rather to seek to "renew justice between government and civil society."

However, it is too limiting to define the appropriate role of government as one of empowerment by steering the resources it controls to nongovernment groups doing good throughout the land. The divine call to government to promote justice requires more robust action than this, as Mary Nelson also urges in her comments.

Indeed, taken on its own logic, the empowerment option undermines itself. The goal of Senator Coats's "agenda of public compassion" is "to break the monopoly of government as a provider of compassion and return its resources to individuals, churches, and charities." But the most direct route to that aim, as the senator's libertarian critics have emphasized, is simply to cut both federal taxation and spending. Why first collect taxes from citizens, removing resources from civil society, only to return them via a tax credit? If it is civil society and not government that holds the secret to constructive solutions to problems, why not leave it up to citizens and nongovernment organizations to decide what to do and how much to spend?

In fact, Senator Coats believes that in their current state of enervation, citizens and civic associations, if left alone, will not adequately respond to the needs of their distressed neighbors. Thus government must compel citizens to do their fair share through its taxation and spending policies, even if it should be civil society and not government that tends to the needy. Yet notice the consequence of this logic: Even after civil society is reinvigorated, government must retain the task of ensuring that the needy receive adequate help and that the institutions of civil society that seek to do well have sufficient resources—that civil society is indeed operating as it should. Government's justice task with regard to civil society thus must go beyond empowerment to monitoring the plight of the powerless and needy and, if necessary, coming to their aid.

Nor is this the full extent of government's justice task in a social policy designed to respect and renew civil society. There is a key enforcement role that cannot be played by civil society: A family abandoned by the father requires not only the loving response of civil society but energetic government action to make the father accept his child support obligations. The institutions of civil society, moreover, depend for their vigor and sustainability in part on government's structuring action: appropriate rules for starting, operating, and ending voluntary associations, for instance, or the rules for entering or dissolving marriage. Further, the health of social institutions rests in part on government's ability and willingness to temper or counteract the forces of the market—for example, by limiting where commercial activities can take place or providing tax breaks to jump-start economic development in inner cities.

In fact, Senator Coats is not blind to these other government tasks. He defends legislation to put boundaries on the Internet to protect families and children. He advocates changes in family law to strengthen the institution of marriage. He has proposed a federal school-choice experiment to help loosen the rigid structures of government-financed education. The problem is that these other constructive and structuring tasks of government are too much overshadowed when government's responsibilities in and to civil society are defined as empowerment, as government assistance to citizens and associations who are doing right and only need additional resources and recognition. To renew justice *between* government and civil society, greater stress should be laid on how government must act *within* and even *against* civil society to vindicate justice.

A Christian Social Philosophy

A key strength of the sphere sovereignty concept to which Senator Coats refers is precisely a stress on the distinct and constructive tasks government must play with regard to civil society. Together with the Catholic teaching of subsidiarity, Abraham Kuyper's notion of sphere sovereignty emphasizes limits on government action, to safeguard the autonomy and scope of action of other institutions within society. This is not a counsel of government noninvolvement; rather, both perspectives urge that government must be active to uphold, not substitute for, the fulfillment of responsibility by social institutions.

The principle of sphere sovereignty goes on to stress the discontinuities between government and civil society, including the distinct actions government must take to complement the responsibilities of social institutions. The tasks of government and civil society are not interchangeable such that the key consideration is which institution is closest to the problem. Moreover, to uphold the social order, government cannot limit itself to transferring resources. It has a whole range of additional critical tasks: constructing the legal frameworks that institutions require, patrolling the boundaries between different institutions and spheres of activity, vindicating justice for people harmed by institutions, safeguarding people within institutions, and promoting the common good—the commonwealth shared by all citizens, which is more than the sum of individuals or social institutions. The principle of sphere sovereignty offers a fuller, more differentiated conception of government support for civil society that can carry us forward in the vital public policy task of restructuring government's relations with society.

Kuyper also intended with the principle of sphere sovereignty to define how a government, ruling over a religiously heterogeneous society, could govern in a way pleasing to God. In fact, he advanced the principle in his 1880 speech inaugurating the Free University of Amsterdam, a Calvinist university to parallel Catholic institutions and the secular universities. What must government do in the face of such religious diversity? Government would dishonor God, Kuyper argued, if it forced all faiths into the private corners of life by refusing to honor equally institutions that proclaim a religious basis and institutions that profess to be secular and nonsectarian. Yet government would equally dishonor God, Kuyper insisted, if it arrogated to itself the authority to decide for all in society who is the true God and then required all to follow by making the institutions of that faith obligatory for everyone. No, what government should do—what it must do, on biblical grounds, in this age between Christ's ascension and his return—is find a way to do justice equally to people and institutions of all faiths. Confessional pluralism—the requirement that government leave the spiritual battle to spiritual weapons—is not a counsel of moderation but a principle of public justice rooted exactly in the biblical guidelines for governments in this age.

Confessional pluralism in practice requires structural pluralism: government limiting itself so nongovernment agencies, each embodying one or another of the philosophies and faiths alive in the nation, can carry out their varied tasks in a holistic way, not required to strip out all moral and spiritual elements so as to be uniform and nonsectarian. Thus, the only way government can, as Senator Coats desires, administer the needed moral medicine to society's ills while honoring the requirement not to coerce the consciences of the citizens is by upholding without religious discrimination the diverse institutions of civil society that are busy responding to social needs.

Kuyper's principle of sphere sovereignty points us in just this direction. What it adds to Senator Coats's public philosophy is the insistence that government's task of upholding civil society is more complex and far-reaching than that of supplying resources to the institutions of civil society. And Kuyper's witness reminds us that the virtues of religious liberty and limited government are grounded not in the founders' blueprint but in the Creator's design.

Senator Dan Coats (R-Ind.) is a graduate of Wheaton College (Ill.) and the University of Indiana School of Law. He practiced law before entering politics and was elected first to the House of Representatives. Senator Coats's primary legislative concern in both houses of Congress has been policies affecting families and children. Known for his leadership in the Project for American Renewal and the Renewal Alliance, the senator has been seeking to change the relation of government to society by means of laws that will strengthen nongovernment institutions.